PYTHON FOR BEGINNERS : LET'S LEARN PYTHON IN 7 DAYS

ABHINAV OJHA

Made with ♥ on the Notion Press Platform
www.notionpress.com

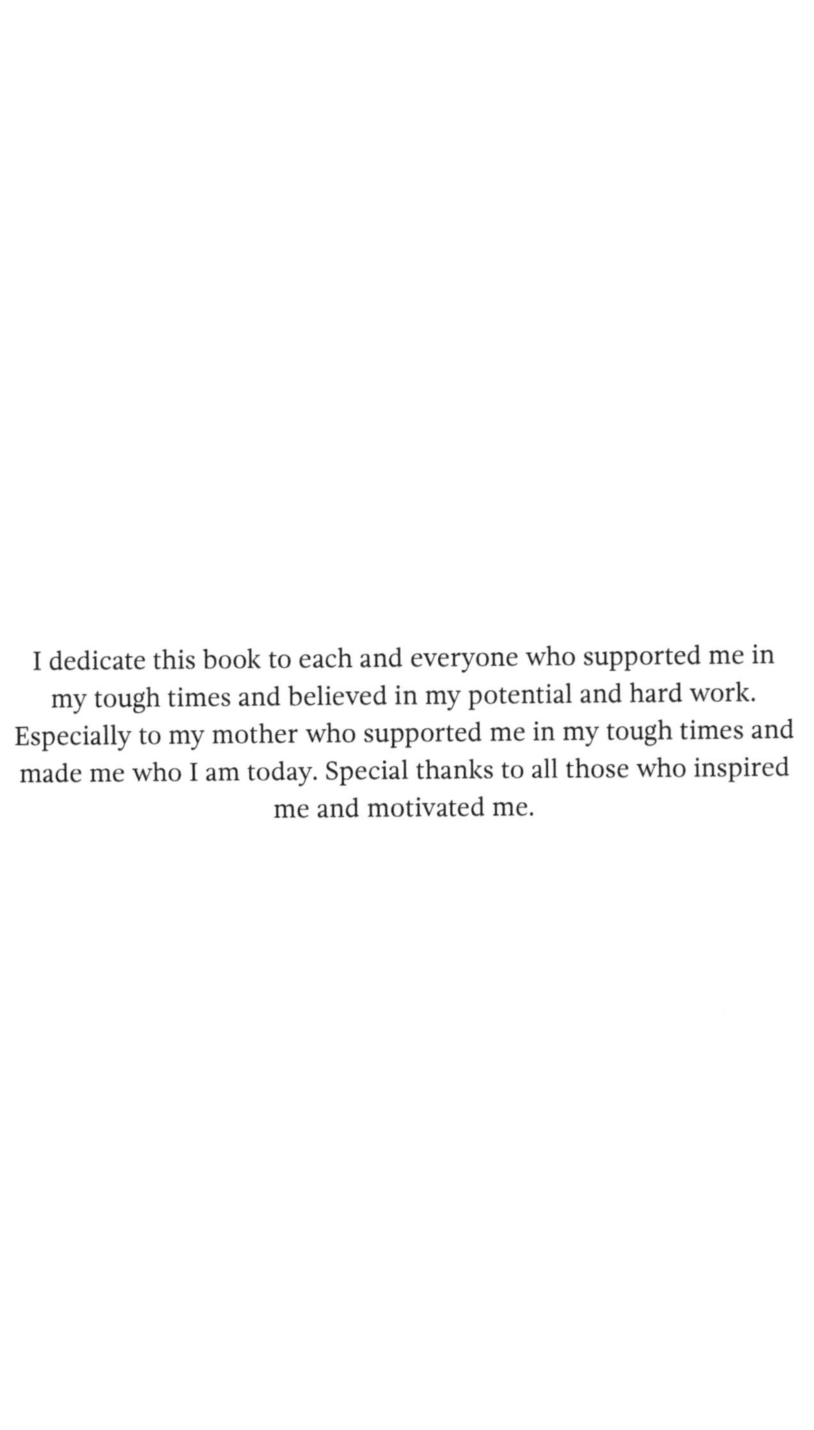

I dedicate this book to each and everyone who supported me in my tough times and believed in my potential and hard work. Especially to my mother who supported me in my tough times and made me who I am today. Special thanks to all those who inspired me and motivated me.

Contents

Contents

Acknowledgements

"I have to start by thanking each and everyone specially my family who supported me so much. From a great failure to all that I have achieved , it can't be achieved without support".

Special thanks to my parents for supporting my dream to become a author and a entrepreneur and all those special people who have directly or indirectly contributed to my success.

Disclaimer And Copyright

Disclaimer

Although the author and publisher have made every effort to ensure that the information in this book was correct at press time, the author and publisher do not assume and hereby disclaim any liability to any party for any loss, damage, or disruption caused by errors or omissions, whether such errors or omissions result from negligence, accident, or any other cause.

All the information provided in this book is merely for educational purposes and information purposes only.

Copyright

All Rights Reserved. This book or any portion thereof may not be reproduced or used in any manner whatsoever without the express written permission of the author or the publisher except for the use of brief quotations in a book review.

About The Author

Abhinav Ojha is one of the youngest ASO and APP marketing experts in the world. An entrepreneur, certified ethical hacker, Programmer, blogger, author, poet, and Founder and CEO of enterstor Private Limited.

Abhinav Ojha is the best-selling author of two books and the overall author of Six books. Abhinav Ojha is an Indian Entrepreneur who has been awarded Five National and One International Award Till now of which include, the **Indian Achievers Award 2020 for Young entrepreneur** and the **Indian Achievers Award for Young Achiever by Indian Achievers Forum**, the **International Achievers award, G town top 50 influential personalities of India 2021** and **young author of the year award, India prime Icon awards etc.**

.

Abhinav has been in the online business since 2016 and runs his own company enterstor private limited. Abhinav Ojha is also an instructor at udemy. Abhinav Ojha is a Software Engineer by Profession. When free, Abhinav likes to grab a coffee and learn more tech.

Social Media Connect

Email:dabhinavojha@gmail.com
    On-Line Chat: www.abhinavojha.com
    Facebook: www.facebook.com/abhinavojhaa
    Instagram: www.instagra.com/abhinavojhaofficial
    Linkedin - https://www.linkedin.com/in/abhinavojhaa/

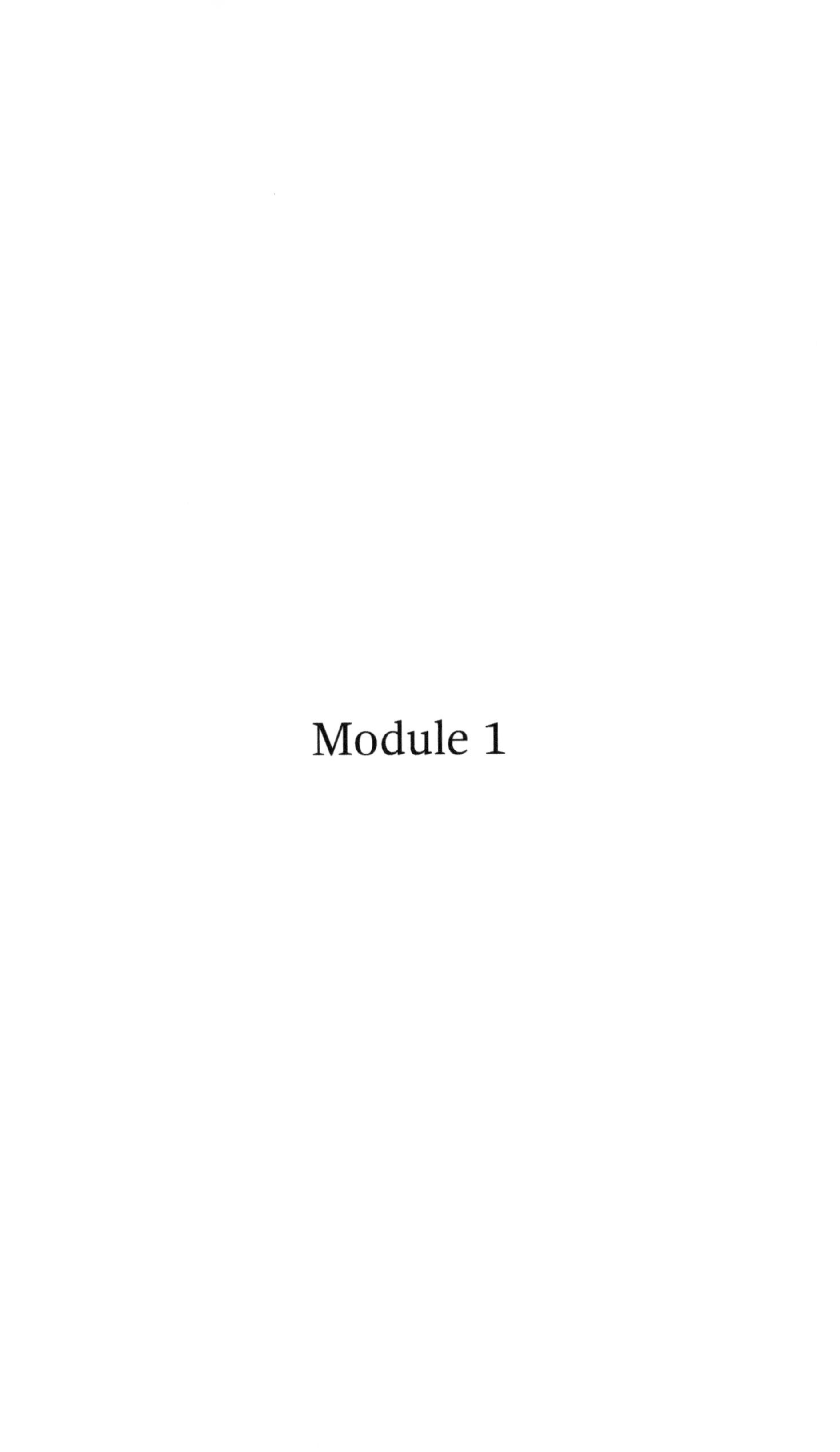

Module 1

## CHAPTER I

History of Python

Python was developed by Guido van Rossum and was first released on February 20, 1991. It was mainly designed to give more flexibility to programmers and its syntax allows programmers to write concepts with fewer lines of code.

According to Wikipedia, Python is a high-level, general-purpose programming language. Its design philosophy emphasizes code readability with the use of significant indentation.

Python is dynamically typed and garbage-collected. It supports multiple programming paradigms, including structured (particularly procedural), object-oriented and functional programming. It is often described as a "batteries included" language due to its comprehensive standard library.

Guido van Rossum began working on Python in the late 1980s as a successor to the ABC programming language and first released it in 1991 as Python 0.9.0. Python 2.0 was released in 2000. Python 3.0, released in 2008, was a major revision not completely backwards-compatible with earlier versions. Python 2.7.18, released in 2020. Python 3.11.1 is the latest stable version of Python at the time of writing this book.

Python consistently ranks as one of the most popular programming languages in 2023.

Why the Name Python?

It's said that Guido van Rossum was reading the script of a popular BBC comedy series named "Monty Python's Flying Circus" in 1970 which ultimately gave him the name Python which was short and at the same time a unique name.

Python is used in almost every technical field such as Artificial Intelligence, Machine Learning, Web Development, App

Development, Web Apps, Hacking etc.

Python Version List

Python 1.0 - released on January 1994.
Python 2.0 - released on 16 October 2000.
Python 3.0 - released on December 2008.
Python 3.5 - released on September 2015
Python 3.7.9 - released on 17 August 2020.
Python 3.7.12 - released on 4 September 2021.
Python 3.11.1 - released on 6 December 2022.

## CHAPTER II

Why Learn Python

Python is one of the most used and easiest languages to learn in 2023. As mentioned earlier, Python is a general-purpose programming language that is widely used to develop websites, Apps, and web apps, also used in data analysis and for ethical hacking tools. The file extension which is used by Python is ".py".

Reasons to Learn Python

1. Easy and Friendly

Python is one of the easiest languages to learn if you are very new to coding. Python uses very simple syntax that uses elements from the natural English Language which makes it easier to read and write. The code uses English keywords instead of punctuations, making it immensely easy to use even for beginners. Unlike others, Python is an interpreted programming language which means you can run each line of code once you have finished writing it which allows you to immediately check and make adjustments to it. We will learn about interpreted and compiled languages in our later chapter.

2. Python is Versatile

Python is versatile which means you can use python for n number of tasks be it app development, or web development. Machine Learning, AI, Game Development, small and other complex tasks.

With more than 137,000 libraries, Python has become one of the most used programming languages in the current era.

Python can also be implemented with other programming languages. A few examples are -

Jython - Python integrated with Java

CPython - Python integrated with C

IronPython - IronPython is an open-source implementation of the Python programming language which is integrated with. NET.

3. High Demand Job Roles

People with skills in Python are most likely to get hired for a job. Python jobs have gained great potential in the last few years and are in great demand for job roles.

There are currently more than 11,000 job advertisements worldwide on Glassdoor for Python-related roles, with Indeed having around 14,000 roles. When you compare the numbers to job roles of other programming languages such as Java, it's almost double.

According to Github, Python continued to see gains in its usage across GitHub with a 22.5% year-over-year increase in 2022.

4. Great Growing Community

Whenever you start with a programming language or the development of a product such as an app, the first thing you want is the community of the people in that field where you can get your errors and questions answered by fellow developers.

Python community size has gone up to 16 Million approx in the year 2023 which makes it easier for the developers to get answers to their errors very easily.

## CHAPTER III

Features and Applications

Python is a case-sensitive language. For example in python, **P** and **p** are treated as two different variables and not the same. Python is also a dynamically typed language where you don't always need to declare the type of variable. Python can also figure out the variable types on its own.

For example

a = 20, here **a** can be anything such as an integer, float or even a string.

For example

a =10 and **b='Python'**, here **a** will be considered as an integer and **b** will be considered as a string.

We will learn about everything in detail in our upcoming chapters.

Before we move forward let's find out some of the features of Python Programming Language.

Features in Python

1. Easy to Learn

Python is one of the easiest languages to learn especially for beginners where no semi-colon and curly braces are used. The indentation itself defines the code block.

2. Fewer lines of Code

Python uses fewer lines of code even to perform complex tasks as compared to other high-level programming languages such as C and Java and hence lowers the development time.

3. Interpreted Language

As mentioned earlier, Python is an interpreted language which simply means that the programme written in python is executed one line at a time.

4. Cross-Platform Language

Python is a cross-platform language which means that the code written for one operating system such as windows will also work in other operating systems such as MAC OS or Linux without any issues.

5. Object-Oriented Language

Python supports the concept of classes and objects, inheritance, polymorphism, encapsulation etc. The OOPs concept allows programmers to reuse code and develop applications in fewer lines of code and eventually lower the development time and period.

6. Large Library

As mentioned earlier, Python has over 1,37,000 libraries which makes the task a lot easier for developers.

A library in short is an already written code for some specific task that can be reused by the developers with ease in their project.

7. GUI Support

GUI stands for Graphical User Interface. GUI is used for developing Desktop Applications. You can develop desktop applications with ease using python with the help of some most used libraries such as PyQT5 and Kivy.

8. Integrated

As mentioned earlier, python can easily be integrated with some other programming languages such as C, C++, Java, etc.

9. Dynamic Memory Allocation

As already mentioned that Python is a dynamically typed language which means you don't need to specify the data type of the variable . Python will identify the data type on its own. When a value is assigned to a variable, it automatically allocates the memory to the variable during run time.

Suppose you want to assign value **50** to the variable **a** then write **a** = **50** rather than writing **int a = 50.**

Applications for Python

1. Web Development

Python can be used for developing websites and Web Apps.
Frameworks such as Django and Pyramid.
Micro-frameworks such as Flask and Bottle.
Advanced content management systems such as Plone and Django CMS.

2. Scientific and Numeric

Python is widely used in scientific and numeric computing:
SciPy is a collection of packages for mathematics, science, and engineering.
Pandas is a data analysis and modelling library.
IPython is a powerful interactive shell that features easy editing and recording of a work session and supports visualizations and parallel computing.

The Software Carpentry Course teaches basic skills for scientific computing, running boot camps and providing open-access teaching materials.

3. Desktop GUIs

The Tk GUI library is included with most binary distributions of Python.

Some toolkits that are usable on several platforms are available separately:

wxWidgets

Kivy, for writing multitouch applications.

Qt via pyqt or pyside

4. Software Development

Python is often used as a support language for software developers, for build control and management, testing, and in many other ways.

SCons for build control.

Buildbot and Apache Gump for automated continuous compilation and testing.

Roundup or Trac for bug tracking and project management.

5. Business Applications

Python is also used to build ERP and e-commerce systems:

Odoo is an all-in-one management software that offers a range of business applications that form a complete suite of enterprise management applications.

Tryton is a three-tier high-level general-purpose application platform.

Other Uses of Python

1. Artificial Intelligence and Machine Learning

2. Data Analytics
3. Data Visualisation
4. Game Development

## CHAPTER IV

Compiler and Interpreter

Compiler

A compiler can be simply stated as a translator that translates a source program written in High-Level Programming languages such as Java, C++ etc into machine language. To make a program executable it's necessary to convert the program into machine language so that the processor understands the program since the processor understands only machine language. In short, it takes the input of High-Level Programming language and produces the output of low-level language which is machine language.

The compiler is relatively slower since it takes a larger part of the memory and goes through the entire program and then translates the program into machine language.

Interpreter

An interpreter can be simply stated as a translator that translates a programming language into comprehensible language.

Instead of going through the entire program and then translating the entire program to machine language as in a compiler, it only translates one statement of the program at a time.

What is Machine Code or Machine Language

A machine code is a language which comprises hexadecimal or binary instructions that computers understand.

Example of Machine Language

Say that a light bulb is controlled by a processor running a program in the main memory. The controller can turn the light bulb fully on and fully off, and can brighten or dim the bulb (but not beyond fully on or off.)

Machine Instruction Machine Operation
00000000 Stop Program
00000001 Turn the bulb fully on
00000010 Turn the bulb fully off
00000100 Dim bulb by 10%
00001000 Brighten bulb by 10%
00010000 If the bulb is fully on, skip over the next instruction
00100000 If the bulb is fully off, skip over the next instruction
01000000 Go to the start of the program (address 0)

Difference between Compiled and Interpreted Language

Compiled Language

A compiled language is a language that is converted into machine language in order to make the program executable.

Examples of compiled languages - are C, C++, C# etc.

Interpreted Language

An interpreted language is a programming language that is interpreted without actually compiling a program into machine language.

Examples - **Python**, Perl, JavaScript
Python is an Interpreted Programming Language.

CHAPTER V

Installing Python and Setting up Environment

In this chapter, we are going to learn step by step guide to downloading and installing Python language interpreter. After installation of Python, we will learn how to use IDLE to write our python programmes.

Python is available for all well-known platforms such as Windows, MAC OS and Linux. You can always visit https://www.python.org/ for more information regarding the same.

How to Install Python on Windows?

1. Visit **https://www.python.org/downloads/**

2. Check for recent releases and click on download.

3. Select **Windows installer (64-bit)** or **Windows installer (32-bit)** to start the downloading process as shown in the below image.

Files

Version	Operating System	Description	MD5 Sum	File Size	GPG	Sigstore		
Gzipped source tarball	Source release		5c986b2865979b393aa50a31c65b64e8	26394378	SIG	CRT	SIG
XZ compressed source tarball	Source release		4efe92adf28875c77d3b9b2e8d3bc44a	19856648	SIG	CRT	SIG
macOS 64-bit universal2 installer	macOS	for macOS 10.9 and later	7c4d83ac21cf1e0470aa133ef6a1fff6	42665618	SIG	CRT	SIG
Windows embeddable package (32-bit)	Windows		cc960a3a6d5d1529117c463ac00aae43	9557137	SIG	CRT	SIG
Windows embeddable package (64-bit)	Windows		f16900451e15abe1ba3ea65713c7fe9e	10538985	SIG	CRT	SIG
Windows embeddable package (ARM64)	Windows		405185d5ef1f436f8dbc370a868a2a85	9763968	SIG	CRT	SIG
Windows installer (32-bit)	Windows		a592f5db4f45ddc3a46c0ae465d3bee0	24054000	SIG	CRT	SIG
Windows installer (64-bit)	Windows	Recommended	3a02deed11f7ff4dbc1188d201ad164a	25218984	SIG	CRT	SIG
Windows installer (ARM64)	Windows	Experimental	3a98e0f9754199d99a7a97a6dacb0d91	24355528	SIG	CRT	SIG

Getting started

4. After downloading the file, run the .exe setup file and install python as shown in the below image. Further click on install python that says includes IDLE, pip and documentation. We will be using IDLE to write our programmes in this book. However, you can also opt for Pycharm and Eclipse IDE.

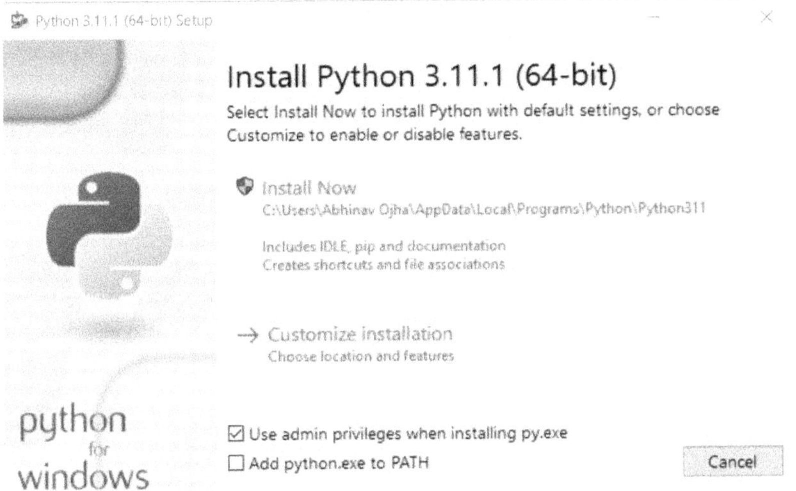

Starting install

5. Let the installation happen automatically.

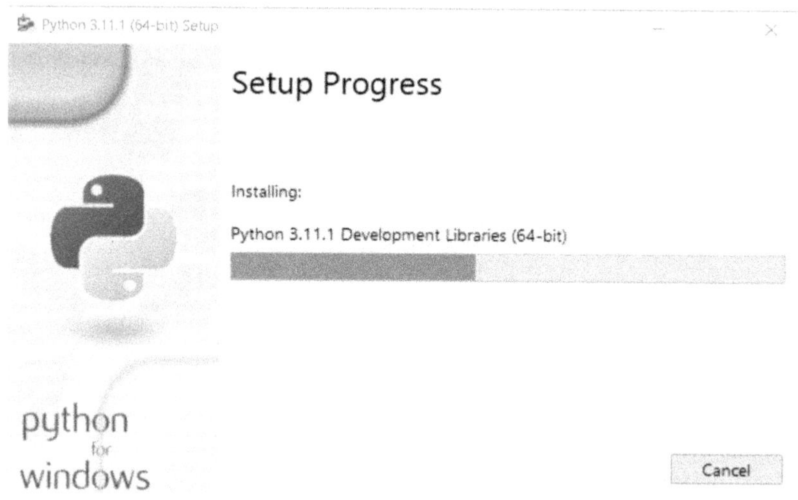

Installing

6. After installation you will find, IDLE is also installed as shown in the below image. We will learn about IDE and IDLE at the end section of this chapter.

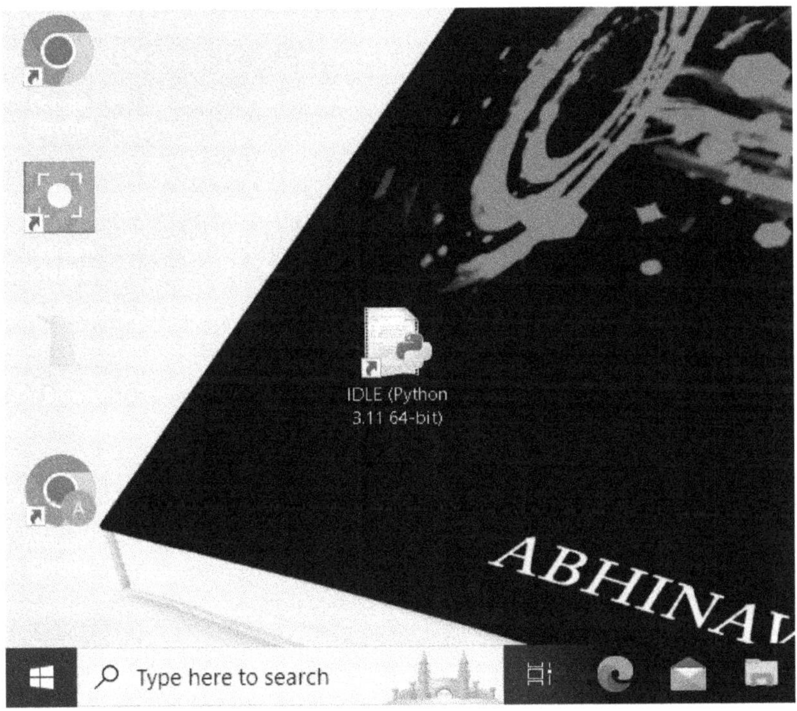

IDLE

7. Now you can write your Python programmes with ease using IDLE Python IDE.

```
Python 3.11.1 (tags/v3.11.1:a7a450f, Dec  6 2022, 19:58:39) [MSC v.1934 64 bit (
AMD64)] on win32
Type "help", "copyright", "credits" or "license()" for more information.
>>>
```

Ln: 3 Col: 0

Writing Programmes

Hope you learned how to install the Python language interpreter and use IDLE.

How to install Python in Linux?

Open the terminal and run the following command.
$ sudo apt-get install python3.8

What is IDE?

IDE stands for Integrated Development Environment which is software that allows developers to build applications in a combination with common development tools and plugins into a single GUI (Graphical User Interface). IDE helps programmers to build applications, edit the source code of a project, build executables and also debugging.

What is IDLE?

According to Python's official website,

IDLE is Python's Integrated Development and Learning Environment.

IDLE has the following features:

coded in 100% pure Python, using the Tkinter GUI toolkit

cross-platform: works mostly the same on Windows, Unix, and macOS

Python shell window (interactive interpreter) with colourizing of code input, output, and error messages

multi-window text editor with multiple undo, Python colourizing, smart indent, call tips, auto-completion, and other features

search within any window, replace within editor windows and search through multiple files (grep)

debugger with persistent breakpoints, stepping, and viewing of global and local namespaces

configuration, browsers, and other dialogs.

Hope now you have learned how to install python and use IDLE as well as basic knowledge about IDE and IDLE.Now we will head on to our next chapter and learn how to write our first basic Python program in IDLE.

## CHAPTER VI

Write your first basic program in Python

Program - Write a Python Program to Find the Average of Two Numbers.

```
a = 20
# First Number
b = 30
# Second Number
average = a + b / 2
# Calculating the Average of Two Numbers
print (average)

#Display Output
    Output = 35.0
```

Program - Write a Python program to calculate Simple Interest Given that P = 9000 , R = 10% and T = 5 years.

```
P = 9000
R = 10
T = 5


SI = P * R * T /100
    # Applying the formula of Simple Interest that is Principle * Rate of Interest * Time Period / 100.

print(SI)
    Output = 4500.0
```

Module 2

## CHAPTER VII

Variables and Data Types

You already wrote your first python program in the previous module, now let's learn about variables and data types in this chapter. We will learn about naming and declaring a variable and about data types.

What are variables?

Variables in short are names given to store data. Once a variable is defined, the program allocates some space in your computer storage to store this data. A variable is created as soon as we assign a value to it. These variables have their own data type. Based on the data type which can be either Integer, Float or string, etc the interpreter allocates memory and decides what kind of data can be stored in these reserved memory locations. Now we can say that a Python variable is a name given to a memory location. The value stored in a variable can always be changed and modified during program execution.

example -

a = 10, where **a** is variable and **10** is the value assigned to the variable.

userAge= 50, where **userAge** is the variable and **50** is the value assigned to the variable.

Assigning values to Variables

In Python, (=) equal sign is used to assign values to the variable. The operand to the left side of the = equal sign is the variable and the operand to the right side of the = equal sign is the value stored in the variable.

Rules for naming variables in Python

1. In python variable names are case-sensitive. **Python** and **python** will be treated as two separate variables.

2. A variable name cannot start with a number.

3. A variable name must start with a letter or the underscore character

4. A variable name can only contain alpha-numeric characters and underscores (A-z, 0-9, and _)

5. The reserved words(keywords) cannot be used to name the variable. (We will learn about keywords in our later chapters).

Example for naming the variables.

userName = "Abhinav"
user_name = "Abhinav"
_user_name = "Abhinav"
USERNAME = "Abhinav"
username2 = "Abhinav"

Not to do while naming a variable in python.

2username = "Abhinav"
user-name = "Abhinav"
user name = "Abhinav"

Multiple Assignment

Python allows the assignment of a single value to more than one variables and multiple values to multiple variables which are separated by commas in a single line as shown below.

```
a=b=c=d=2000
e,f,g = "Abhinav","John","Rock"
print(f)
John
print(d)
2000
```

Multiple Assignment

Output :

John

2000

In the first case. value 2000 is assigned to multiple variables such as a, b, c and d which is known as **(many-to-one)**.

In the second case, multiple values such as "Abhinav", "John" and "Rock" are assigned to multiple variables e,f, g in a single line which is known as **(many-to-many)**.

Important Note - To create a string, put the sequence of characters inside either single quotes, double quotes, or triple quotes and then assign it to a variable. I recommend you always use double quotes whenever you assign a string to a variable otherwise using single quotes when there is an Apostrophe in the string can cause errors.

From the above examples you can definitely notice that In Python, unlike statically typed languages like C or Java, there is no need to specifically declare the data type of the variable. In dynamically typed languages such as Python, the interpreter itself predicts the data type of the Python Variable based on the type of value assigned to that variable.

## CHAPTER VIII

Data Types

Data Types

Every variable has a data type. For example, **userAge = 50**, where **50** is a number which is a **numeric data type** referred to as **Integer**. Same way n= **20.5** where **20.5 is a decimal value** which is a **float data type** and **name** = "Peter" is a **string data type.**

There are different types of data types in Python. Some built-in Python data types are:

Numeric - int, float and complex.
Sequence Type - string, list and tuple.
Boolean
Set
Dictionary

Numeric Data Type

In python, the numeric data type represents the data type that has a numerical value. The numerical value can either be an Integer without any decimal or a float with decimals or even a complex number.

Integers – This value is represented by int class. It contains positive or negative whole numbers (without fractions or decimals).

Float – This value is represented by the float class. It is a real number with a floating-point representation. It is specified by a decimal point.

Complex Numbers – Complex number is represented by a complex class. It is specified as (real part) + (imaginary part)j. For example – 2+3j

example -

```
x=10
print(type(x))
<class 'int'>
```

Integers

Output:
<class 'int'>

```
x=10.5
print(type(x))
<class 'float'>
```

Float

Output:
<class 'float'>

```
x=2+3j
print(type(x))
<class 'complex'>
```

Complex

Output:
<class 'complex'>

Python supports four different numerical types. They are -

1. int (integer value)
    2. float (floating point real values)
    3. long (long integers, they can also be represented in hexadecimal and octal)
    4. complex (complex numbers)

Sequence Type

Strings

A string can be defined as a sequence of characters or a collection of more than one character put in a single quote, double quote or triple quote. A string is represented by the **str** class.
    example -

```
course = "Let's learn Python for Beginners"
print(type(course))
<class 'str'>
```

Strings

Output:
<class 'str'>

Strings in python have the below operators.

Slice Operator ([] and [:]): By using the slice operator ([] and [:]) with indexes starting at 0 in the beginning of the string and working their way from -1 at the end, subsets of the string can be taken.

 ex -

```
course = "Let's learn Python for Beginners"
print(course[2])
t
```

Slice Operator

Output:
t

 Plus (+) sign operator: This operator is used to concatenate or add two or more strings.

example -

```
book = "Let's learn python for Beginners"
author = "Abhinav Ojha"
print("book"+"author")
bookauthor
```

Example One

Output:

bookauthor

In the above example, you can see the output is bookauthor instead of Let's learn python for Beginners Abhinav Ojha. It happened because we have used print("book" + "author") where book and author both are treated as strings since it's enclosed within double quotes rather than a variable hence the output bookauthor.

```
book = "Let's learn Python for Beginners"
author = "Abhinav Ojha"
print(book+author)
Let's learn Python for BeginnersAbhinav Ojha
```

Example Two

Output:
Let's learn Python for BeginnersAbhinav Ojha

Here we have used print(book+author) and not any single or double quotes hence the strings in the variables are added and the output is Let's learn Python for BeginnersAbhinav Ojha.

Asterisk (*) sign operator: This operator is used to multiply the strings by a number of times.

example :

```
author="Abhinav Ojha"
print(author*5)
Abhinav OjhaAbhinav OjhaAbhinav OjhaAbhinav OjhaAbhinav Ojha
```

Asterisk(*) Operator

Output:

Abhinav OjhaAbhinav OjhaAbhinav OjhaAbhinav OjhaAbhinav Ojha

Lists

Lists can be considered the same as arrays (*An array is a collection of items of the same data type stored at contiguous memory locations*) which is an ordered collection of data. But a list is flexible as the items in the list do not need to be of the same type. A list contains items which are separated by commas and enclosed within square brackets([]). The only difference between arrays and lists in python is that arrays cannot have different data types for elements while lists can have different data types for elements.

example :

```
list = [10 , 20.5 , "Abhinav"]
print(list)
[10, 20.5, 'Abhinav']
```

Lists Example

You can see in the above example that all the elements in the above-created list have different data types.**10 is Integer, 20.5 is float** and **"Abhinav" is a string.**

Lists in python have the below operators.

Slice Operator ([] and [:]): By using the slice operator ([] and [:]) with element position starting at 0 in the beginning of the list and working their way from -1 at the end, subsets of the list can be taken.

example -

```
list = [10 , 20.5 , "Abhinav"]
print(list[2])
Abhinav
```

Slice Operator ([] and [:]):

Output:

Abhinav

Here Abhinav is the output since the element is indexed at position 2.

```
list = [10 , 20.5 , "Abhinav"]
print(list[1:2])
[20.5]
```

Example Two

Output:

(20.5,)

Here 20.5 is the output since print(list[1:2]) will print elements starting from 1st till 2nd. Please note that till the second element will not print the second element.

```
list = [10 , 20.5 , "Abhinav"]
print(list[1:])
[20.5, 'Abhinav']
```

Example Three

Output:

(20.5, 'Abhinav')

Here (20.5, 'Abhinav') is the output since print(list[1:]) will print elements from index position 1 to the end element.

Plus (+) sign operator: This operator is used to concatenate or add two or more Lists.

```
listone = [10 , 20.5 , "Abhinav"]
listtwo = ["Python" , 50 , "Author"]
print(listone+listtwo)
[10, 20.5, 'Abhinav', 'Python', 50, 'Author']
```

Adding Two Lists

Output:

(10, 20.5, 'Abhinav', 'Python', 50, 'Author')

Asterisk (*) sign operator: This operator is used to multiply the lists by a number of times.

```
list = [10 , 20.5 , "Abhinav"]
print(list*2)
[10, 20.5, 'Abhinav', 10, 20.5, 'Abhinav']
```

Lists Multiply

Output:

(10, 20.5, 'Abhinav', 10, 20.5, 'Abhinav')

Tuples

Tuples are like lists but the only difference between tuple and list is that tuples cannot be modified after it has been created while lists can be modified after creation. It is represented by the tuples class.

Tuples are enclosed in **parenthesis(())** while **lists** are enclosed in brackets **([])**.

The elements and size of a tuple cannot be modified while lists can be modified.

```
tuple = (10 , 20.5 , "Abhinav " , "Books")
print(tuple)
(10, 20.5, 'Abhinav ', 'Books')
```

Tuples

Tuples in python have the below operators.

Slice Operator ([] and [:]): By using the slice operator ([] and [:]) with element position starting at 0 in the beginning of the tuple and working their way from -1 at the end, subsets of the tuples can be taken.

```
tuple = (10 , 20.5 , "Abhinav" , "Books")
print(tuple[3])
Books
print(tuple[1:3])
(20.5, 'Abhinav')
print(tuple[1:])
(20.5, 'Abhinav', 'Books')
```

Tuples - **Slice Operator ([] and [:])**

Output

Books - Element at 3ʳᵈ index position.

(20.5, 'Abhinav') - Elements from index position 1 to index position 3 but not 3.

(20.5, 'Abhinav', 'Books') - Elements from index position 1 to the end element.

Plus (+) sign operator: This operator is used to concatenate or add two or more Tuples.

```
tupleone = (10, 20.5 , "Abhinav" , "Books")
tupletwo = ("Let's learn python for beginners" , "by Abhinav Ojha" )
print(tupleone+tupletwo)
(10, 20.5, 'Abhinav', 'Books', "Let's learn python for beginners", 'by Abhinav Ojha')
```

Adding Tuples

Output

(10, 20.5, 'Abhinav', 'Books', "Let's learn python for beginners", 'by Abhinav Ojha')

Asterisk (*) sign operator: This operator is used to multiply the tuples by a number of times.

```
tupleone = (10 , 20.5 , "Abhinav " , "Books")
print(tupleone*2)
(10, 20.5, 'Abhinav ', 'Books', 10, 20.5, 'Abhinav ', 'Books')
```

Multiply Tuple

Boolean Data Type

The boolean data type has one of the two built-in values i.e **True** or **False**. You can evaluate any expression in python and get one of the two answers that is **True** or **False**. When two values are compared, Python returns the Boolean answer as True or False.

example -

```
print(20>10)
True
print(10>20)
False
```

Boolean Example

```
a = True
print(type(a))
<class 'bool'>
```

Boolean Example

***Important Note -True** and **False** with capital **T** and Capital **F** are valid booleans otherwise Python will throw an error if you type it in small letters.*

Sets

In python, a set is an unordered collection of data that is iterable, mutable and has no duplicate elements. There are basically two types of sets in python, one is a **set** and the other one is a **frozen set**. The difference between a set and the frozen set is that the **former**

is mutable which means you can modify a set but the latter is **not mutable** so it cannot be modified once created. However, we will focus on sets only and not on frozen sets.

Creating Sets

Sets can be created by using the built-in set() function with an iterable object or a sequence by placing the sequence inside curly braces, separated by a comma.

Here are some of the features of sets in Python:

Duplicate items are not allowed. If any elements appear multiple times, only one will be considered in the set.

The items in a set are unordered. The order of the set changes every time it is used.

Example of Sets -

```
setone = set([ 1 , 10 , 5 , 2 , 55 , 15])
print(setone)
{1, 2, 5, 10, 15, 55}
```

Sets

Output:

(1, 2, 5, 10, 15, 15)

You can notice in the above example that the output is all ordered in ascending order.

No Duplicate Elements

```
settwo = set([ 1 , 10 , 5 , 5 , 2 , 2, 55 , 15])
print(settwo)
{1, 2, 5, 10, 15, 55}
```

Duplicate Elements

Output:

(1, 2, 5, 10, 15, 55)

In the above example, you can notice that set two contains 5 and 2 two times which is not printed in the output result. As we already know that any duplicate items in the sets will be considered as only one item.

Set of Strings

```
setthree = set(["Abhinav" , "Ojha" , "Author"])
print(setthree)
{'Ojha', 'Author', 'Abhinav'}
```

Set of Strings

Output:

('Ojha', 'Author ', 'Abhinav')

In the above example, You'll notice that when the set consisting of string elements was printed out, the values appeared in a different order. This is one of the features of sets in Python.

Dictionary

A dictionary in python is an unordered collection of data values, which is used to store values in **key: value** pairs. Each key: value pair in a dictionary is separated by a colon: while each key is separated by a 'comma'.

Creating a Dictionary

A dictionary can be easily created in Python by placing a sequence of elements within curly braces separated by commas.

Important Points for Creating a Dictionary

1. Values in a dictionary can be of any data type and can also be duplicated.

2. Keys in a dictionary cannot be repeated or duplicated.

3. Dictionary can also be created using the built-in function dict().

Example -

```
mydictionary = { "brand" : "BMW" , "model" : "X5" , "year" : 2023 }
print(mydictionary)
{'brand': 'BMW', 'model': 'X5', 'year': 2023}
```

Dictionary Example One

```
mydictionary = { "brand" : "BMW" , "model" : "X5" , "year" : 2023 }
print(mydictionary)
{'brand': 'BMW', 'model': 'X5', 'year': 2023}
print(mydictionary["model"])
X5
```

Dictionary Example Two

With this we have come to end of our Data Types Chapter , this was just an basic knowledge of Data types in python , we will learn about Strings , Lists , Tuples , Sets and Dictionary in details in our Module 3 of this book.

## CHAPTER IX

Input() Function

43

Input Function() in Python

Input() funtion is used to take input from the user in Python. By default , it returns the user input in form of a **string** .However if any user wants to take input as int or float , we need to typecast it .We will learn about typecasting in detail in our next chapter.

Example of input() funtion.

```
x = input("What is your name ")
y = input("What is your age")
print(x)
print(y)
```

input() funtion

Output:

What is your name John
What is your age25
John
25

Taking Two Integers from users as input and adding them.

```python
x = int(input("Enter First Number "))
y = int(input("Enter Second Number"))
z = x+y
print(z)
```

using int()

Output:

Enter First Number 10
Enter Second Number40
50

## CHAPTER X

Type Casting

Type Casting in Python

Type Casting in short can be defined as the process of **converting one data type of the variable** to **another data type.**The conversion can be from **int to float** , **int to string** , **string to int** , **float to int** , and **string to float** and **float to string.**We will learn about type casting in python through examples.

Types of Type Casting

There are two types of type casting -

   1.Implicit Type Casting - In implicit Type Conversion , Python automatically converts one data type to another data type in order to get the relevant output.

   2.Explicit Type casting - In Explicit Type Conversion , nothing is done automatically .Programmers are involved in converting one data type to another in order to get the relevant output.

Data Type Functions()

int() - Int() funtion takes **float or string** as an **arguemnet** and returns int type object.

   float() - float() funtion takes **int or string** as an **arguement** and returns float type object.

   str() - str() funtion takes **float or int** as an **arguement** and returns string type object.

What is an arguement?

Any information that are passed into a function can be termed as an arguement.In other words , an arguement is a value that is passed to a function when it is called.

Implicit Type Conversion Example

```
a = 20
print(type(a))
<class 'int'>
b= 10.5
print(type(b))
<class 'float'>
c = a+b
print(c)
30.5
print(type(c))
<class 'float'>
```

Implicit Type Conversion

From the above example , we can learn that a = 20 which is an interger value while b = 10.5 which is a float value and c=a+b which gave us 30.5 which is a float value , so we have added interger value with a float value which gave us the result in a floating value that is 30.5 , so you can see when we print type of c , Python has automatically converted int data type to float data type .

Explicit Type Conversion Example

Type Casting from int to float

```
a = 20
print(type(a))
<class 'int'>
b = float(a)
print(b)
20.0
print(type(b))
<class 'float'>
```

Type casting int to float

Output :

<class 'int'>

20.0

<class 'float'>

Type Casting from float to int

```
a = 10.9
print(type(a))
<class 'float'>
b = int(a)
print(b)
10
print(type(b))
<class 'int'>
```

Type casting float to int

Output :

<class 'float'>

10

<class 'int'>

Type Casting from int to string

```
a = 10
print(type(a))
<class 'int'>
b = str(a)
print(b)
10
print(type(b))
<class 'str'>
```

Type casting int to string

Output :

<class 'int'>

10

<class 'str'>

More Example of Type Casting in Python

```
birth_year = input_("Enyer your birth year")
current_year = 2023
your_age = current_year - birth_year
print(your_age)
```

Error in Program - cannot substract **string value** from a
interger value.

Output:

```
Enyer your birth year1997
Traceback (most recent call last):
  File "C:\Users\Abhinav Ojha\PycharmProjects\pythonProject\main.py", line 3, in <module>
    your_age = current_year - birth_year
               ~~~~~~~~~~~~~^~~~~~~~~~~~~
TypeError: unsupported operand type(s) for -: 'int' and 'str'

Process finished with exit code 1
```

Output

We know that whenever we take a **input** from user it returns
the value in **form of a string** , so here in the above example we
have taken **birth_year as input** from the user and **current year
is a integer value** so when we are substracting **current_year -
birth_year** to get **your_age** , we are getting an error only because
you cannot substract **string value** from a **interger value.**Here **Type
casting comes into place** , we will type cast the string value into
an interger by **using int()** and then get our output as shown in the
below example.

```
birth_year = input_("Enyer your birth year")
current_year = 2023
your_age = current_year - int(birth_year)
print(your_age)
```

Type Casting string to Int

Output:

```
Enyer your birth year 1997
26

Process finished with exit code 0
```

Output

From the above program , you can notice that we converted **birth_year** taken as input from the user which returned an **string to int by using int()** and then we substract both the integer values **current_year- birth_year** to get the **your_age** and we got out **output as 26** instead of a error.

## CHAPTER XI

Operators and Operands

Operator

Operators can be defined as special symbols that perform operations on variables or that manipulate the value of operands.
Let me show you an example for better understanding -

20 - 5 = 15

Here - **(subtraction)** is known as the **operator** and **20 and 5** are known as **operands.**

Types of Python Operators

In Python, the following are the operators.

1. Arithmetic operators
2. Assignment Operators
3. Comparison Operators
4. Logical Operators
5. Bitwise Operators
6. Special Operators

1.Arithmetic Operators

Arithmetic operators are used to performing mathematical operations like addition, subtraction etc.
    + **(used for addition)**, for example, **10 + 5 = 15**
    - **(used for subtraction)**, for example, **10 - 5 = 5**

* (used for multiplication), for example, **10 * 5 = 50**
/ (used for division), for example, **10/5 = 2**
//(used for floor division), for example **10//3 = 3**
%(used for Modulo), for example **5%2 = 1**
(used for Power), for example **42 = 16**

Example -

```python
a = 10
b = 5
print(a+b)    #Addition
print(a-b)    #Substraction
print(a*b)    #Multiplication
print(a/b)    #Division
print(a//b)   #Floor Division
print(a%b)    #Modulus
print(a**b)   #Power
```

Arithmetic Operators

Output:

```
15
5
50
2.0
2
0
100000
```

Output

2.Assignment Operator

Assignment operators are used to assigning values to variables.

for example **a = 5**

here = is an **assignment operator** that assigns value 5 to the variable a.

Let's see the list of different assignment operators in Python.

= (**assignment operator**), for example, **a = 10**

+ = (**addition assignment**), for example, **a + = 5** will be same as **a = a + 5**

- = (**subtraction assignment**), for example, **a - = 5** will be same as **a = a - 5**

* = (**multiplication assignment**), for example, **a * = 5** will be same as **a = a * 5**

/ = (**division assignment**), for example **a / = 5** will be same as **a = a / 5**

% = (**remainder assignment**), for example **a % = 10** will be same as **a = a % 10**

** = (exponent assignment), for example **a ** = 10** will be same as **a = a ** 10**

3.Python Comparision Operator

The comparison operator compares two values and a boolean that is either **True or False.**

Let's see the list of different comparison operators in Python.

= = (**Is Equal To**), for example, **10** = = **10** gives us True

! = (**Not Equal To**), for example, 10! = 5 gives us True

> (**Greater Than**), for example, 2 > 5 gives us False

< (**Less Than**), for example, 2 < 5 gives us True

>= (**Greater Than or Equal To**), for example, 3>= 5 gives us False

<= (**Greater Than or Equal To**), for example, 3<= 5 gives us True

Example -

```
a = 10
b = 5
print(a==b)
False
print(a!=b)
True
print(a>b)
True
print(a<b)
False
print(a>=b)
True
print(a<=b)
False
```

Comparison Operators

4.Python Logical Operator

Logical Operators in Python are used to check whether an expression is True or False.

Let's see the list of different logical operators in Python.

and (a and b), meaning, **True** only if **both the operands are True**

or (a or b), meaning, **True** if at **least one of the operands** is **True**

not (not a), meaning, **True** if the **operand is False and vice-versa.**

Example -

```
a = 5
b = 10
print((a<b) and (b>a))
True

print((a<b) or (b<a))
True

print((a>b) or (b>a))
True

print((a>b) or (b<a))
False
```

Logical Operators

5.Bitwise Operators

Bitwise operators act on operands as if they were strings of binary digits. They operate bit by bit, hence the name bitwise operator.

Let's see the list of different bitwise operators in Python.

&(Bitwise AND) for example , x & y = 0 (0000 0000)

| (Bitwise OR) for example , x | y = 14 (0000 1110)

~ (Bitwise NOT) for example ,~x = -11 (1111 0101)

^ (Bitwise XOR) for example , x ^ y = 14 (0000 1110)

>> (Bitwise right shift) for example , x >> 2 = 2 (0000 0010)

<< (Bitwise left shift) for example , x << 2 = 40 (0010 1000)

6.Special operators

Python offers some special types of operators such as the identity operator.

In Python, **is** and **is not** being used to check if two values are located on the same part of the memory. Two variables that are equal do not imply that they are identical.

is, True if the operands are identical that is they refer to the same object then **x is True.**

is not, True if the operands are not identical that is they do not refer to the same object then **x is not True.**

## CHAPTER XII

Loops

Let me define you what a Loop is? When a program is executed , it runs sequentially that is it runs in a sequence which simple means the statement which appears first in the sequence is executed first and then the next statement and so on till the last statement of the written program.

But sometimes we need to run the same block of code multiple times in a program and hence loops are required.Loops are basically a controlled structure that allows us to run the same block of code multiple times in a progran if the condition is true or else exit the loop if the condition is false.A block of code is basically a statement or group of statements.

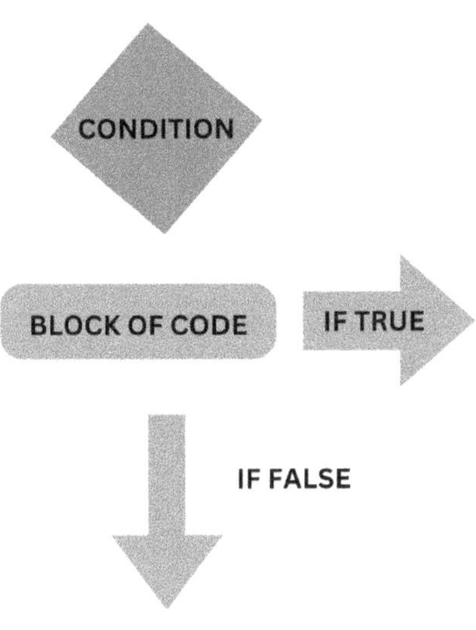

Loops

Different Types of Loops in Python

There are different types of loops used in Python , they are While Loop , For Loop and Nested Loop.

1.While Loop - Python while loops are categorized under indefinite iteration that means it's not specified how many times a python while loop will execute.

Python while loop is used to execute a statement or a block of statement repeatedly until a given condition is satisfied.The line after the loop in a program is executed when the condition becomes false.

2.For Loops - Python for loop executes a sequence of statements multiple times.

3.Nested Loops - Nested loop is a loop within a loop.In short , in python we can use while loop inside another while loop or for loop or for loop inside another while loop or for loop.

Loop Control Statements in Python

In order to change the execution from its normal sequence we use Loop control statements in python such as break , continue or pass statement.When these executions leaves a scope , all automatic objects that were created in that scope are either destroyed or removed.

1.Break statement - Break statement in python is used to terminate the loop statement and the execution is transfered to the statement just after the end of the loop.

2.Continue statement - In python, the continue statement is used to skip a particular iteration of a loop when a specific condition is met.When a continue statement is executed inside a loop, it skips the current iteration of the loop and jumps to the next iteration.

3.Pass statement - The pass statement is a placeholder statement that does nothing.In Python we use pass statement when a statement is required syntactically but we do not want any command or code to be executed.

Loops Examples in Python

1.While Loop

```
1   i=0
2   while(i<3):
3       print('The current count is',i)
4       i=i+1
5   print('Done with while loop')
```

While loop in Python

Output:
The current count is 0
The current count is 1
The current count is 2
Done with while loop

2.For Loop

```
1   fruits = ["Apple" , "Mango" , "Banana"]
2   for index in range(len(fruits)):
3       print("The current fruit:",fruits[index])
4   print("Done with for loop")
```

For Loop in Python

Output:
The current fruit: Apple
The current fruit: Mango
The current fruit: Banana
Done with for loop

3.Nested Loop

```
1  count1=0
2  while(count1<3):
3      count2=0
4      while(count2<3):
5          print('Current values for count1 is ', count1 , 'and count2 is'
                  ,count2)
6          count2=count2+1
7      count1=count1+1
8  print("Done with nested while loop")
```

Nested Loop

Output:
Current values for count1 is 0 and count2 is 0
Current values for count1 is 0 and count2 is 1
Current values for count1 is 0 and count2 is 2
Current values for count1 is 1 and count2 is 0
Current values for count1 is 1 and count2 is 1
Current values for count1 is 1 and count2 is 2
Current values for count1 is 2 and count2 is 0
Current values for count1 is 2 and count2 is 1
Current values for count1 is 2 and count2 is 2
Done with nested while loop

## CHAPTER XIII

Dicision making and expressions

Python programming requires decision-making statements because they let programs decide what to do and run distinct code blocks according to predefined conditions.Programmers can control how a program executes depending on a variety of conditions by using these statements such as if , elif and if-else.

Python Programming language provides these decision making statements.They are :

1.**if statement** : if statement consists of a boolean expression which is usually followed by one or more statements.

2.**if....else statement** : if statement can also be followed by else statement which is optional and which executes only when the boolean expression is false.

3.**nested if statement** : You can use one if or else if statement inside another if or else if statements.

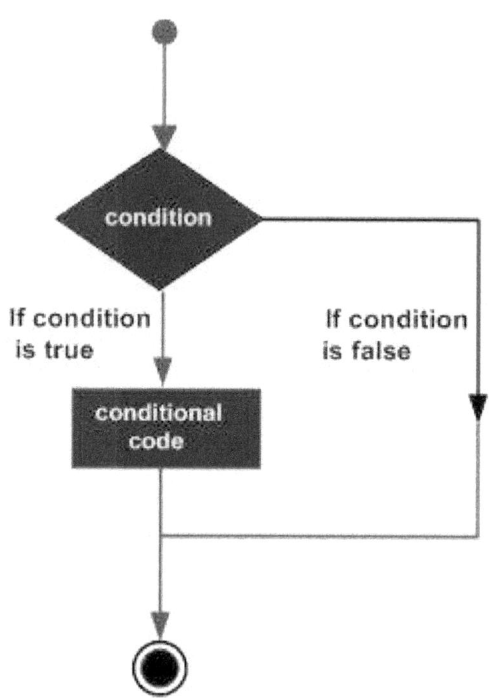

Decision making

Keywords such as if...elif...else is used in python decision making.The if keyword requires a boolean expression i.e True or False followed by colon (:).Further the colon(:) symbol starts an indented block.The statement which has same level of indentation are executed if the boolean expression is True.If its False then the interpreter bypasses the indented block and proceeds to execute statements at earlier indentation level.

*We have already learnt about indentation in our initial chapters.

Example of if statement :

```
num = 20
```

```
if num > 0
print ("the number is a positive number ")
```

Example of if else statement :

```
num = 20
if num % 2 ==0:
print ("Even no ")
else:
print("Odd no")
```

Example of Nested if else statement in Python :

```
num = 20
if num > 0:
if num % 2 == 0;
print("The no is positive and also even ")
else:
print("The number is positive but odd no ")
else:
print("The no is not positive")
```

Hopefully you understood how decision making works in Python.

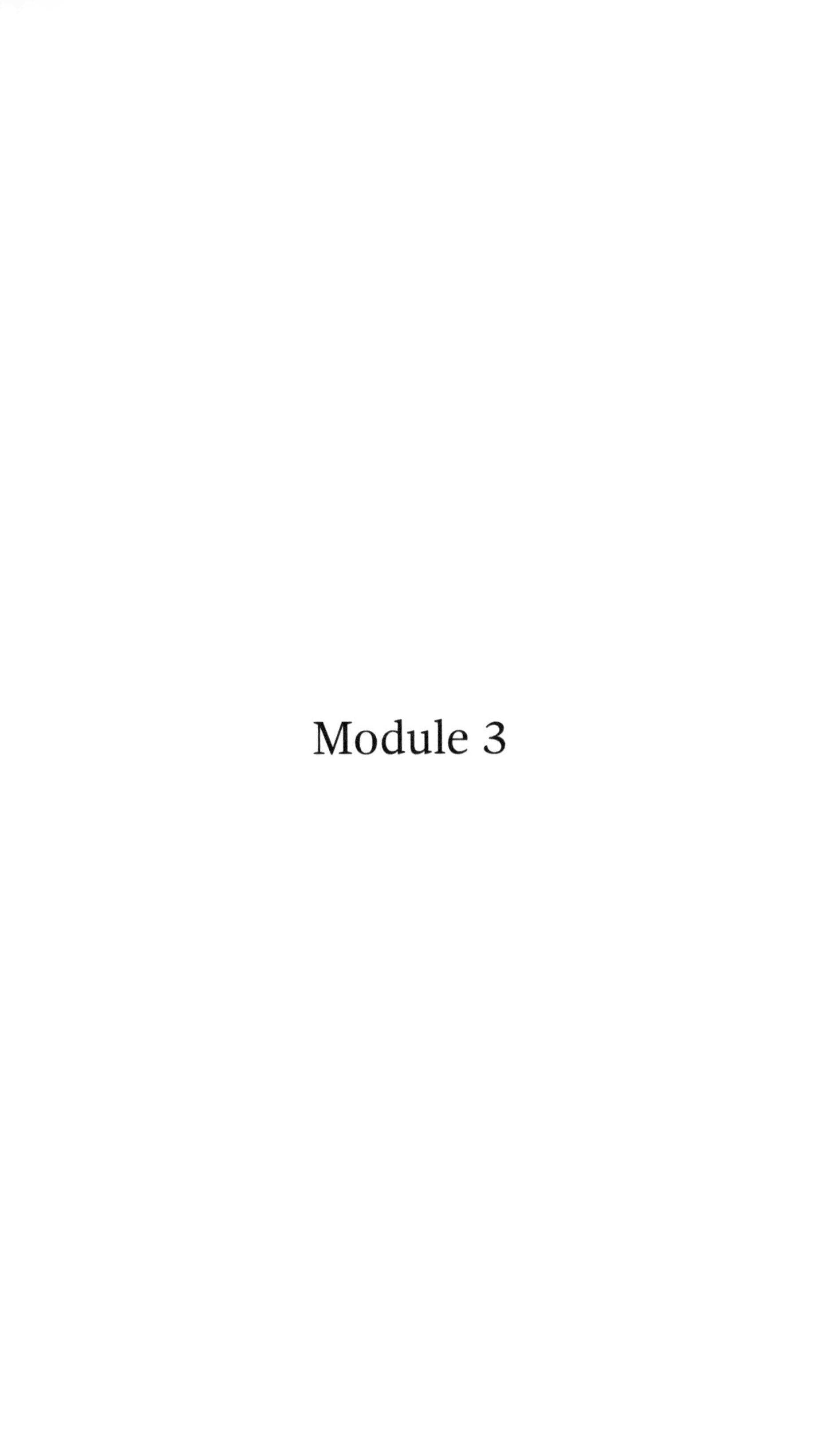

Module 3

## CHAPTER XIV

Keywords in Python

Keyword Description

and - A logical operator

as - To create an alias

assert - For debugging

break - To break out of a loop

class - To define a class

continue - To continue to the next iteration of a loop

def - To define a function

del - To delete an object

elif - Used in conditional statements, same as else if

else - Used in conditional statements

except - Used with exceptions, what to do when an exception occurs

False - Boolean value, result of comparison operations

finally - Used with exceptions, a block of code that will be executed no matter if there is an exception or not

for -To create a for loop

from - To import specific parts of a module

global - To declare a global variable

if -To make a conditional statement

import - To import a module

in -To check if a value is present in a list, tuple, etc.

is - To test if two variables are equal

lambda - To create an anonymous function

None - Represents a null value

nonlocal - To declare a non-local variable

not - A logical operator

or -A logical operator

pass - A null statement, a statement that will do nothing

raise - To raise an exception

return - To exit a function and return a value

True - Boolean value, result of comparison operations

try - To make a try...except statement

while - To create a while loop

with - Used to simplify exception handling

yield - To end a function, returns a generator

## CHAPTER XV

Lists

WE have already learnt about lists in our previous chapters.Let's learn about lists in some details.WE already know that Lists can be considered the same as arrays (*An array is a collection of items of the same data type stored at contiguous memory locations*) which is an ordered collection of data. But a list is flexible as the items in the list do not need to be of the same type. A list contains items which are separated by commas and enclosed within square brackets([ ]). The only difference between arrays and lists in python is that arrays cannot have different data types for elements while lists can have different data types for elements.

In this chapter we will learn about creating and Modifying Lists.

Creating a List

Suppose we need to record the ages of 5 students. Instead of creating 5 separate variables, we can simply create a list.

```
1  ages = [ 18 , 20 , 25 , 24 , 19]
2  print(ages)
3
```

Creating a list

Output:
[18, 20, 25, 24, 19]

#All the elements are printed inside the list.

Accessing List Elements

```
1   cars = ["Maruti" , "Tata" , "Honda"]
2   print(cars[0])
3   print(cars[1])
4   print(cars[2])
5
```

Accessing List Elements

Output:
Maruti
Tata
Honda
Explaination -
#Maruti is at index position 0 , Tata is at index position 1 and Honda is at index position 2.

Negative Indexing

Python allows negative indexing , for example -1 will refer to the last element in the list while -2 will refer to the second last item in the list.Same way -3 will refer to the third last item in the list.

```
1   cars = ["Maruti" , "Tata" , "Honda"]
2   print(cars[-1])
3   print(cars[-2])
4
```

Negative Indexing

Output:
Honda
Tata

Adding Elements to a List

We have already learnt that lists are mutable that is it can be modified and changed once created.WE can use different methods to add items to a list.

1.append() method - This method adds a new item at the end of the list.

2.extend() method - We use the extend() method to add all the items of an iterable (list, tuple, string, etc.) to the end of the list.

3.insert() method - This method is used to add a new element to the list at any specified index position.

Examples -

1.Using append()

```
1   students = ["Abhinav" , "Akash" , "Ankit" , "Soham"]
2   print(students)
3   students.append("Utsav")
4   print(students)
5   |
6
```

Adding elements Using append()

Output:
['Abhinav', 'Akash', 'Ankit', 'Soham']
['Abhinav', 'Akash', 'Ankit', 'Soham', 'Utsav']
   #Utsav is added at the end of the list using append() method.

2.Using extend()

```
1   numbers = [2 , 4 , 6 , 8 , 10]
2   odd_numbers = [1 , 3 , 5 , 7 , 9]
3   numbers.extend(odd_numbers)
4   print(numbers)
5
6
```

Adding elements Using extend()

Output:
[2, 4, 6, 8, 10, 1, 3, 5, 7, 9]
#odd_numbers are added to numbers.

3.Using insert()

```
even_numbers = [ 2 , 4 , 8 , 10]
even_numbers.insert(2,6) #Here 6 will be inserted at index positon 2
print(even_numbers)
```

Inserting items in the list

Output:
[2, 4, 6, 8, 10]
#6 was inserted at index postion 2 by using insert() method.

Changing Lists Items

```
cars = ["Maruti" , "Tata" , "Honda"]
cars[1] = "BMW"
print(cars)
```

Changing Lists Items

Output:
['Maruti', 'BMW', 'Honda']
#"Tata" which was located at index position 1 was replaced by
"BMW"

Removing items from the List

WE can remove items from a list by using del statement or by using remove() method.

Using del statement and remove() method

```
cars = ["Maruti" , "Tata" , "Honda"]
del cars[1]
print(cars)
cars.remove("Honda")
print(cars)
```

Using del statement and remove() method

Output:
['Maruti', 'Honda']
['Maruti']
    #del cars[1] deleted the item present at index postion 1 which is "Tata".
    #cars.remove("Honda") deleted the item "Honda" from the list.

Length of Lists

```
cars = ["Maruti" , "Tata" , "Honda"]
size = len(cars)
print(size)
```

Length of Lists

Output:

3

#There are three strings present in the list hence the length of the list is 3.

Let us now about list methods in Python.

Method Description
append() - add an item to the end of the list
extend() - add all the items of an iterable to the end of the list
insert() - inserts an item at the specified index
remove() - removes item present at the given index
pop() -returns and removes item present at the given index
clear() -removes all items from the list
index() -returns the index of the first matched item
count() -returns the count of the specified item in the list
sort() -sort the list in ascending/descending order
reverse() -reverses the item of the list
copy() -returns the shallow copy of the list

## CHAPTER XVI

Tuples

WE have already learnt in our previous chapters that Tuples are like lists but the only difference between tuple and list is that tuples cannot be modified after it has been created while lists can be modified after creation. It is represented by the tuples class.

Tuples are enclosed in **parenthesis(())** while **lists** are enclosed in brackets **([])**.

The elements and size of a tuple cannot be modified while lists can be modified.

In this chapter we will learn about creating and Modifying Lists.

Creating a Tuple

```python
your_tuple = () #Creating empty tuple
print(your_tuple)


ages = (20, 25, 30 , 35 , 40) #Creating tuple having integers
print(ages)



mixed_tuple = (10, 20.5 , "Hello Students") #with mixed datatypes
print(mixed_tuple)
```

Creating Tuple

Output:

()
(20, 25, 30, 35, 40)
(10, 20.5, 'Hello Students')

Accessing Tuple Elements

```
vowels = ("a" , "e" , "i" , "o" , "u")
print(vowels[1])
print(vowels[4])
```

Accessing tuple elements

Output:

e

u

Explaination -

print(vowels[1]) will print "e" since it is present at index position 1.

print(vowels[4]) will print "u" since it is present at index position 4.

Negative Indexing

WE have already learnt that Python allows negative indexing , for example -1 will refer to the last element in the list while -2 will refer to the second last item in the list.Same way -3 will refer to the third last item in the list.

```python
vowels = ("a" , "e" , "i" , "o" , "u")
print(vowels[-1])
print(vowels[-4])
```

Negative Indexing

Output:
u
e

Explaination -
print(vowels[-1]) will print "u" since negative indexing starts from the end and "u" is the last item in the tuple.So -1 will print "u".

print(vowels[-4]) will print the fourth last item in the tuple that is "e".

Slicing

```python
vowels = ("a" , "e" , "i" , "o" , "u")
print(vowels[1:4]) #Prints ('e', 'i', 'o')
print(vowels[:-1]) #Prints ('a', 'e', 'i', 'o')
```

Slicing

Output:
('e', 'i', 'o')
('a', 'e', 'i', 'o')

Explaination -

print(vowels[1:4]) will print all the items starting from index postion 1 to 3 that is it will print "e" , "i", "o".Please note that items present at index position 4 will not be printed.

print(vowels[:-1]) will print ('a', 'e', 'i', 'o') . : this means it will start from the first item in the tuple which is at index position 0 and will print till -1 which is "u" but will not print "u".

Python Tuple Methods

We already know that tuples cannot be modified once created hence there is no adding and removing of items in the tuple.

Unlike Lists ,methods that add items or remove items are not available with tuple. Only the following two methods are available which as shown below.

```python
your_tuple = ('a', 'e', 'a', 'l', 'e', 'm', 'n', 'a')

print(your_tuple.count('a'))
print(your_tuple.index('e'))
```

Tuple Methods

Output:

3

1

Explaination -

print(your_tuple.count('a')) will count how many times "a" is present in the tuple and will print the output.In this case 'a' is present 3 times hence the output is 3.

print(your_tuple.index('e')) will print the index postion of the item "e" in the tuple.In this case the index position of "e" is 1 , hence the output is 1.WE know that index position starts from 0.

## CHAPTER XVII

Dictionary

WE have already learnt in our previous chapters that A dictionary in python is an unordered collection of data values, which is used to store values in **key: value** pairs. Each key: value pair in a dictionary is separated by a colon: while each key is separated by a 'comma'.

Creating a Dictionary

We create dictionaries by placing key:value pairs inside curly brackets {}, separated by commas.

```python
1  indian_state_capitals = {          #Creating Dictionary
2    "Jharkhand": "Ranchi",
3    "Karnataka": "Banglore",
4    "Tamil Nadu": "Chennai",
5    "West Bengal": "Kolkata",
6  }                                   #Printing Dictionary
7  print(indian_state_capitals)
```

Creating a Dictionary

Output:

{'Jharkhand': 'Ranchi', 'Karnataka': 'Banglore', 'Tamil Nadu': 'Chennai', 'West Bengal': 'Kolkata'}

Python Dictionary Length

WE can find the length of the dictionary by using the len() function.

```
1  indian_state_capitals = {
2      "Jharkhand": "Ranchi",
3      "Karnataka": "Banglore",
4      "Tamil Nadu": "Chennai",
5      "West Bengal": "Kolkata",
6  }
7  print(len(indian_state_capitals))
```

Python Dictionary Length

Output:

4

Add Items to a Dictionary

To add items to the Dictionary , follow the below example

```
1  indian_state_capitals = {
2      "Jharkhand": "Ranchi",
3      "Karnataka": "Banglore",
4      "Tamil Nadu": "Chennai",
5      "West Bengal": "Kolkata",
6  }
7  indian_state_capitals["Assam"] = "Dispur"
8  print(indian_state_capitals)
```

Add Items to a Dictionary

Output:

{'Jharkhand': 'Ranchi', 'Karnataka': 'Banglore', 'Tamil Nadu': 'Chennai', 'West Bengal': 'Kolkata', 'Assam': 'Dispur'}

Remove Items to a Dictionary

We use the del statement to remove an element from the dictionary

```
indian_state_capitals = {
    "Jharkhand": "Ranchi",
    "Karnataka": "Banglore",
    "Tamil Nadu": "Chennai",
    "West Bengal": "Kolkata",
}
del indian_state_capitals["West Bengal"]
print(indian_state_capitals)
```

Remove Items to a Dictionary

Output:

{'Jharkhand': 'Ranchi', 'Karnataka': 'Banglore', 'Tamil Nadu': 'Chennai'}

Python Dictionary Methods

Function Description

    pop() Remove the item with the specified key.

    update() Add or change dictionary items.

    clear() Remove all the items from the dictionary.

    keys() Returns all the dictionary's keys.

    values() Returns all the dictionary's values.

    get() Returns the value of the specified key.

    popitem() Returns the last inserted key and value as a tuple.

    copy() Returns a copy of the dictionary.

Module 4

OOPS, Concept in Python

## CHAPTER XVIII

OOP Concept in Python

Before we start to learn the OOPs (Object-oriented programming) concept in Python. Let's understand what OOP and POP are.

What is POP?

POP stands for Procedure-Oriented-Programming, which in short is a method that uses functions to break down tasks in a systematic approach and each task is completed in an order. It focuses on the functions or procedures that are needed for the computation, rather than the data itself.

In short, the POP approach uses a sequence of instructions to break down the programs into functions and each task is completed in an order. The global data or variables are shared by these functions and data is easily exchanged between them.

Here are some examples of procedural-oriented programming (POP) languages:

C, Pascal, FORTRAN, BASIC, COBOL, and ALGOL.

Some characteristics of POP.

1. It follows a step-by-step approach and each task is completed in an order.

2. Programs are broken down into functions, which are basically smaller blocks of code.

3. Data can be easily exchanged between one function to another and at any time from any location.

4. It follows a top-down programming approach.

What is OOP?

OOP stands for Object-oriented programming. As the name states, OOP is a computer programming paradigm that relies on the concept of classes and objects.OOP is a programming paradigm that organizes software design around data rather than functions and logic.OOP is a high-level programming concept that divides the larger programs into objects and each object is a data filled with its own behavior and set of properties.

Programming languages that support OOP are Java, C++, JavaScript and Python.

Note : Programming paradigm is a technical term used to describe the structure and elements of a computer program.

Advantages of OOP :

1.OOP makes it very easier to maintain and modify code.

2.OOP provides a clear program structure.

3.OOP programs are executed faster.

4.OOP program codes can be reused easily, and the project can be coded with less lines of code which also decreases the development time of the project.

5.OOP is suited to big, complicated and frequently updated or maintained projects.

The difference between OOP and POP?

DIFFERENCE BETWEEN OOP AND POP

91

OOP	POP
It deals with objects and classes.	It deals with functions and procedures.
Bottom to Up Approach	TOP to Down Approach
Data can be hidden	Data cannot be hidden
Method overloading and overriding are used in OOPS	Functions or procedures can't take multiple forms

The difference between OOP and POP

## CHAPTER XIX

Concepts of OOPS

There are six major concepts of OOP (Object-Oriented Programming) and they are as follows :
1. Class
2. Objects
3. Inheritance
4. Polymorphism
5. Abstraction
6. Encapsulation

1. Class

In short, a Class is a template that defines the methods and variables for a specific type of object. A class is a user-defined data type that acts as a blueprint for creating objects that have their own set of properties and behavior. It is defined using the 'class' keyword followed by the name of the class and a pair of curly braces. A class contains real values instead of variables.

1. A class can have subclass that can inherit some or all of the characteristics of the main class.

2. Subclasses can also define their own methods and methods that are not there in the main class.

3. The structure of a class and its subclasses is called class hierarchy.

2. Objects

An object is an instance of a class created with specific data. It holds real data and interacts with other objects through methods. Each object has its own unique properties and behavior. Objects are created using classes which define their structure and once it is instantiated, objects can operate independently but can interact through defined interfaces by following encapsulation and abstraction. It enhances the reusability of the code and also maintaining the code for larger projects that are maintained and updated regularly.

Characteristics of an Object in OOPs.

Let's consider there is an object called student.

1. **State** : Name, Age, Gender, Address, Height, Weight.
2. **Behavior** : Reading, Writing, Running.
3. **Identity** : IDcard, RollNO, RegNo.
4. **Responsibility** : To study well and score pass marks, score good marks, become the topper.

3. Inheritance

Inheritance allows one class (subclass or child class) to inherit some or all properties and methods from another class, also known as the parent class or main class. Inheritance promotes code reusability, allowing developers to build larger applications without rewriting the same lines of code.

The best example to define inheritance is 'father and son" i.e. genetics.

You are the child of your parents, and you might have some similar traits like the 'same eye color, same height, same body type, etc. that you have inherited from your father or your mother. At the same time, you can also have your own traits that's unique to you, for example, you can be taller than your father or shorter than your father. Here you are the "**child class**" that has inherited some attributes and behavior from the '**parent class**' that is your father.

4. Polymorphism

Polymorphism grants a special ability to object to function to take multiple forms. In OOP, polymorphism allows the methods to behave differently in different scenarios depending on the object that is calling it. Polymorphism in short refers to the use of the same function name, but with different signatures, for multiple types.

Method Overloading :

This allows multiple methods of the same class to have the same name but different parameters.

Method Overriding :

When a subclass or a child class provides its own implementation of a method inherited from the main class or parent class, then it's known as method overriding.

5. Abstraction

Abstraction in OOPs in short can be defined as the process of hiding complex and internal details of an application from the user and exposing only the necessary parts of the object to the user. It focuses on what an object does, rather than how it's implemented and how it does it. It creates a boundary between the application and the client.

For example, let us consider you are withdrawing cash from the ATM.

For that purpose, you will insert your ATM card or debit card in the ATM, enter the PIN, input the withdrawal amount, and you will receive the cash in your hand along with a receipt that will display your current balance and withdrawal amount along with ID. However, there were a lot of backend process involved while you're withdrawing the cash such as the bank received the request, the bank amount was fetched and then withdrawn and the current balance was updated, and you did not have to worry about anything as this process was done in the backend.

This is what we call Polymorphism in OOP, It only displays the information that is necessary for the user, hiding all the complex and implementation details that are not required.

6. Encapsulation

In short, Encapsulation limits direct access to some of the data. It is the process of wrapping data (variables) and the methods (functions) that operate into a single unit, known as a class. Encapsulation as stated restricts direct access to some of the components of an object and bundles them together.

Encapsulation promotes the concept of data hiding and data security, as the internal representation of an object is hidden from the outside world and access to the data is only allowed through defined methods that are "getters and setters". Encapsulation hides data and methods, which can prevent other developers from using the code.

What is a Constructor?

Constructor has the same name, that of a class. In (OOP), a constructor is a special function that initializes an object when it's created. Constructors are automatically called when an object of a class is instantiated. Constructors don't have any return type

## CHAPTER XX

OOPs in Python

Class and Objects in Python

Before we proceed to learn about Class and Object in Python, let me share you a real-world example for the same.

Let us consider a class **Person**

Class Person

**A Person has some State and Behavior
State : Name, Gender, Profession, Height
Behavior : Working, Studying**

Object 1 : Aarav

State :

Name : Aarav

Gender : Male

Profession : Software Engineer

Height : 175 cm

Behavior :

Working : He works as a Software developer in one of the Top MNC's.

Studying : He studies 5 hours a day.

Object 2 : Suhani

State :

Name : Suhani

Gender : Female

Profession : CA

Height : 162 cm

Behavior :

Working : She works as a CA in one of the Top MNC's.

Studying : He studies 8 hours a day.

As you can see, Here, both **objects Aarav and Suhani** are created from the same **class Person**, but they have different **states and behaviors.**

Using the above class Person, we can create multiple objects that depict different states and behavior.

Create a class in Python.

Example 1:

```
class Person :
Statement 1
Statement 2
Statement 3
Statement N
```

Example 2 :

```
class Dog:
def __init__(self, name, age):
self.name = name
self.age = age

def bark(self):
print(f"{self.name} says woof!")
```

Here in this example :
*woof is the barking sound made by the Dog.
We have created a class called Dog.
__init__ method is used to initialize the state of the object.
self is a parameter that is used to reference the current instance of the class and access its variables.

Objects in Python

When we create an object in Python, an instance of the class is created that is complete with attributes and methods.

Class Dog

Objects : Dog 1, Dog 2, Dog 3, Dog 4

State : Name, Age

Behavior : Bark, Sleep

How Create Objects For the Class Dog

```
dog1 = Dog("Bailey", 2)
dog2 = Dog("Daisy", 4)
dog3 = Dog("Josh", 5)
dog4 = Dog("Max", 6)
```

How to Access Class Attributes Using Objects

print(dog1.name)
print(dog2.age)
print(dog3.name)
print(dog4.age)

The Whole Python Program and its Output :

```python
class Dog:
    def __init__(self, name, age):
        self.name = name
        self.age = age

    def bark(self):
        print(f"{self.name} says woof!")

# Creating objects

dog1 = Dog("Bailey", 2)
dog2 = Dog("Daisy", 4)
dog3 = Dog("Josh", 5)
dog4 = Dog("Max", 6)

# Accessing attributes
print(dog1.name)
print(dog2.age)
print(dog3.name)
print(dog4.age)


# Modifying attributes

dog1.age = 6
print(dog1.age)

dog2.name = "Charlie"
print(dog2.name)

dog3.age = 2
print(dog3.age)


dog4.name = "Bella"
print(dog4.name)

# Calling methods

dog1.bark()
dog2.bark()
```

Python Class and Object

Program :

```
class Dog:
def __init__(self, name, age):
self.name = name
self.age = age


def bark(self):
print(f"{self.name} says woof!")
```

Creating objects

```
dog1 = Dog("Bailey", 2)
dog2 = Dog("Daisy", 4)
dog3 = Dog("Josh", 5)
dog4 = Dog("Max", 6)
```

Accessing attributes

```
print(dog1.name)
print(dog2.age)
print(dog3.name)
print(dog4.age)
```

Modifying attributes

```
dog1.age = 6
print(dog1.age)


dog2.name = "Charlie"
print(dog2.name)


dog3.age = 2
print(dog3.age)



dog4.name = "Bella"
print(dog4.name)
```

Calling methods

```
dog1.bark()
dog2.bark()
```

Output :

```
Bailey
4
Josh
6
6
Charlie
2
Bella
Bailey says woof!
Charlie says woof!
```

Module 5

Python Programs

## CHAPTER XXI

Program 1

Program 1 : Write a program to calculate the factorial of a number in Python using a FOR loop.

What is a factorial of a number?

A factorial, in mathematics, is the product of all positive integers less than or equal to a given positive integer and denoted by that integer and an exclamation point. Thus, factorial seven is written 6!, meaning $1 \times 2 \times 3 \times 4 \times 5 \times 6 = 720$.

```python
n = int (input (" Please Enter a number: "))

#Taking Input (integer ) from the user which will be stored in variable n

factorial = 1

# Lets Say the user has taken 5 as Input

if n >= 1:

    # As user has taken 5 as input so the value stored in n is 5 and it is
        # greater than 1 hence we will execute the for loop now

            for i in range (1, n+1):

                # Now the loop will run from 1 to n+1..and the value stored in i will be 1 , 2 , 3 4 , 5 , 6

                    factorial = factorial *i


                        # Now we will get the factorial of the no as the value stored in factorial is 1
                        # and i is from 1 to 6 hence the loop will run till 5
                        #  and it will be executed as 1*2*3*4*5 and the output will be 120


print ("Factorial of the given number is: ", factorial)
```

Write a program to calculate the factorial of a number in
Python using a FOR loop.

EXPLANATION :

n = int (input (" Please Enter a number: "))

#Taking Input (integer) from the user which will be stored in variable n

factorial = 1

 # Lets Say the user has taken 5 as Input

if n >= 1:

 # As user has taken 5 as input so the value stored in n is 5 and it is
greater than 1 hence we will execute the for loop now

for i in range (1, n+1):

 # Now the loop will run from 1 to n+1..and the value stored in i will be 1 , 2 , 3 4 , 5 , 6

*factorial = factorial *i*

 # Now we will get the factorial of the no as the value stored in factorial is 1
 # and i is from 1 to 6 hence the loop will run till 5
*# and it will be executed as 1*2*3*4*5 and the output will be 120*

print ("Factorial of the given number is: ", factorial)

Output :

Please Enter a number: 5
The factorial of the given number is: 120

## CHAPTER XXII

Program 2

Program 2 : Python Program to check if a given year is a Leap year or Not.

What is Leap Year?

A leap year is a year that is divisible by 4 but not by 100, unless it is also divisible by 400. Leap years have an extra day, February 29th, instead of the usual 28 days.

```python
year = int(input("Enter a year you want to check "))

# Taking integer input from the user

if year % 4 == 0:
    if year % 100 == 0:
        if year % 400 == 0:

            # % is known as the modulus operator, also known as the remainder operator,
            # it divides two numbers and returns the remainder.

            # We know that a leap year is a year that is divisible by 4 but not by 100, unless it is also divisible by 400.

            print("The year you entered is a leap year!")
        else:
            print("The year you entered is not a leap year!")
    else:
        print("The year you entered is a leap year!")
else:
    print("The year you entered is not a leap year!")
```

Python Program to check if a given year is a Leap year or Not.

EXPLAINATION :

year = int(input("Enter a year you want to check "))

Taking integer input from the user

if year % 4 == 0:
if year % 100 == 0:
if year % 400 == 0:

% is known as the modulus operator, also known as the remainder operator,
it divides two numbers and returns the remainder.

We know that a leap year is a year that is divisible by 4 but not by 100, unless it is also divisible by 400.

print("The year you entered is a leap year!")
else:
print("The year you entered is not a leap year!")
else:
print("The year you entered is a leap year!")
else:
print("The year you entered is not a leap year!")

Output :

Enter a year you want to check

2024
The year you entered is a leap year!

Output :

Enter a year you want to check

2000
The year you entered is a leap year!

Output :

Enter a year you want to check

2015
The year you entered is not a leap year!